For the boys—Mark, Brady, and Scott

Published by Derrydale Books,
Distributed by Outlet Book Company, Inc.,
a Random House Company,
40 Engelhard Avenue
Avenel, New Jersey 07001

Printed and bound in China

Library of Congress Cataloging-in-Publication Data
Hughes, Joleen.
Things!   1994 : CIP   t.p.   (Joleen Hughes)
p.   c.m.
ISBN 0-517-10151-3
1. English Language—Rhyme—Juvenile literature.
2. Vocabulary—Juvenile literature. [1. English language—Rhyme.
2. Vocabulary.]   I. Title.
PE1517.H84   1994
428.1—dc 20   93-44877
CIP
AC
8 7 6 5 4 3 2 1

THINGS!

RHYMES AND PICTURES BY JOLEEN HUGHES

Derrydale Books
New York • Avenel

A · BOOK

AND · A · HOOK

A · HAT

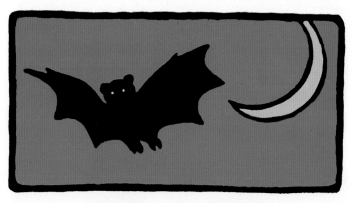

AND · A · BAT

A · STAR

AND · A · CAR

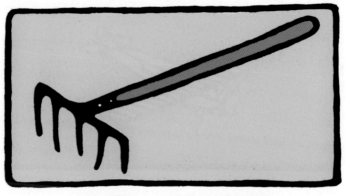

AND · A · RAKE

A · PLANE

AND · A · TRAIN

A · CLOCK

AND · A · BLOCK

A · BUG

AND · A · RUG

AND · A · CAKE

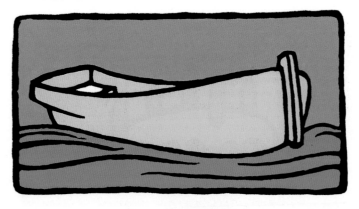

A · BOAT

AND · A · COAT

A · MOON

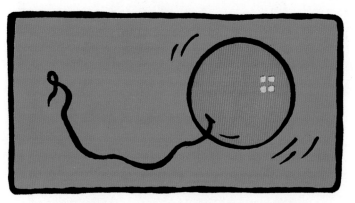

AND · A · BALLOON

A · CHAIR

AND · A · PEAR

AND · A · TOWN

A · TREE

AND · A · KEY

A · PHONE

AND · A · BONE

A · SLED

AND · A · BED

AND · A · CROWN

PHONE

BOOK

BUG

CLOCK

CHAIR

STAR

BED

COAT

CROWN

PEAR

RAKE

HAT

TREE

CAR

BALLOON